BOOK WORMS

Math Around Us

Neighborhood Math

Dawn James

Cavendish
Square

New York

Published in 2015 by Cavendish Square Publishing, LLC
243 5th Avenue, Suite 136, New York, NY 10016

Copyright © 2015 by Cavendish Square Publishing, LLC

First Edition

Website: cavendishsq.com

This publication represents the opinions and views of the author based on his or her personal experience, knowledge, and research. The information in this book serves as a general guide only. The author and publisher have used their best efforts in preparing this book and disclaim liability rising directly or indirectly from the use and application of this book.

CPSIA Compliance Information: Batch #WW15CSQ

All websites were available and accurate when this book was sent to press.

Library of Congress Cataloging-in-Publication Data

James, Dawn, author.
Neighborhood math / Dawn James.
pages cm. — (Math around us)
Includes index.
ISBN 978-1-50260-155-1 (hardcover) ISBN 978-1-50260-154-4 (paperback) ISBN 978-1-50260-153-7 (ebook)
1. Counting—Juvenile literature. 2. Arithmetic—Juvenile literature. 3. Neighborhoods—Juvenile literature. I. Title.

QA113.J37 2015
513.2—dc23

2014032626

Editor: Amy Hayes
Copy Editor: Cynthia Roby
Art Director: Jeffrey Talbot
Designer: Douglas Brooks
Senior Production Manager: Jennifer Ryder-Talbot
Production Editor: David McNamaraa
Photo Researcher: J8 Media

The photographs in this book are used by permission and through the courtesy of: Cover photo by Fertnig/Getty Images; Salvator Barki/Getty Images, 5; Robert Houser/UpperCut Images/Getty Images, 7; kali9/E+/Getty Images, 9; LWA/Photographer's Choice/Getty Images, 11; © iStockphoto.com/joebelanger, 13; Image Source/Photodisc/Getty Images, 15; Hero Images/Hero Images, 17; Cade Martin/UpperCut Images, 19; Take A Pix Media/Blend Images/Getty Images, 21.

Printed in the United States of America

Contents

Exploring the **neighborhood** is fun.

How many windows does this house have?

This house has **2** windows.

5

Jim holds his dad's hand when they cross the street.

How many people cross the street?

3 people cross the street.

5 kids wait for the **school bus**.

3 kids get on the bus.
How many kids are left?

2 kids are left.

Some families walk their dogs in the neighborhood.

How many people are in this family?

4 people and **1** dog are in this family.

Sidewalk chalk comes in many colors.

There are **6** pieces of chalk.

How many are yellow?

1 piece of chalk is yellow.

13

There are **3** kids drawing with the chalk.

If **3** more kids came to draw, how many kids would there be?

There would be **6** kids drawing with the chalk.

Ice cream trucks bring ice cream to the neighborhood.

2 kids want vanilla ice cream and **2** kids want chocolate.

How many kids want ice cream?

4 kids want ice cream.

Kayla had **2 scoops** of ice cream.

She ate **1**. How many scoops does Kayla have left?

She has **1** scoop left.

How many kids sit on the stoop?

There are **3** kids sitting on the stoop.

Math in the neighborhood sure is fun!

21

New Words

ice cream trucks (ISE CREEM TRUX) Trucks that drive around to sell ice cream.

neighborhood (NAY-bor-hood) A section of a town or city.

school bus (SKOOL BUS) A vehicle that takes children to and from school.

scoops (SKOOPS) The amount held by a large spoon called a scoop.

sidewalk chalk (SYDE-walk CHALK) Chalk used for drawing on cement.

Index

About the Author

Dawn James loves taking photographs and going to baseball games. She lives in Pittsburgh, PA.

About BOOKWORMS

Bookworms help independent readers gain reading confidence through high-frequency words, simple sentences, and strong picture/text support. Each book explores a concept that helps children relate what they read to the world they live in.